Editor
Kim Fields

Managing Editors
Karen Goldfluss, M.S. Ed.
Ina Massler Levin, M.A.

Editorial Project Manager
Mara Ellen Guckian

Illustrator
Kelly McMahon

Cover Artist
Barb Lorseyedi

Art Manager
Kevin Barnes

Art Director
CJae Froshay

Imaging
Craig Gunnell
Rosa C. See

Publisher
Mary D. Smith, M.S. Ed.

Author

Traci Ferguson Geiser, M.A.

Teacher Created Resources, Inc.
6421 Industry Way
Westminster, CA 92683
www.teachercreated.com
ISBN-1-4206-3140-3

©2005 Teacher Created Resources, Inc.
Made in U.S.A.

Table of Contents

Introduction 3

How to Use This Book 4

Teddy Bears (*Colors*)

Poem 5

Unit Activities 6

Home/School Connection 8

Pocket Chart Cards 10

Picture Cards 20

Student Poem Page 22

Mini Book 23

Leaves (*Uppercase and Lowercase Letters*)

Poem 28

Unit Activities 29

Home/School Connection 31

Pocket Chart Cards 33

Picture Cards 38

Student Poem Page 40

Mini Book 41

Leafy Letters 46

Pumpkins (*Sequencing—Size*)

Poem 51

Unit Activities 52

Home/School Connection 54

Pocket Chart Cards 56

Picture Cards 61

Student Poem Page 63

Mini Book 64

The Nut Hunt (*Recognizing Numbers*)

Poem 69

Unit Activities 70

Home/School Connection 72

Pocket Chart Cards 74

Number Words 82

Picture Cards 84

Student Poem Page 86

Mini Book 87

Squirrel Patterns 92

Nut Patterns 93

Apples (*Rhyming*)

Poem 94

Unit Activities 95

Home/School Connection 97

Pocket Chart Cards 99

Picture Cards 105

Student Poem Page 107

Mini Book 108

Introduction

A Poem in My Pocket: Fall was designed to provide busy teachers with hassle-free, developmentally appropriate literacy experiences for young children. All of the activities included in each unit will help develop prereading skills and give children fun, hands-on experiences with print. Phonological awareness skills, such as rhyming, syllabication, and beginning and ending sounds, will be focused on throughout the lessons. Students will review lines of poetry, observing sentences and punctuation. Further, they will have opportunities to point out the words forming each sentence and note the syllables (and phonemes) used to make different words.

The *Poem in My Pocket* series consists of three seasonally themed books: *Fall, Winter,* and *Spring.* The books include five units, each containing a full week of thematic lesson plans based on an original poem. The *Fall* book incorporates the following themes: Teddy Bears, Leaves, Pumpkins, The Nut Hunt, and Apples.

Each unit includes the following components:

Original Poem: Each poem in the book was created to enhance the topics typically explored in preschool and kindergarten. Each poem can be enlarged to display in the classroom or copied to create a book of poetry for your classroom library. These simple poems will complement your existing curriculum and help build oral language skills. Reproducible Pocket Chart Cards and Picture Cards are included for each poem and require minimal teacher preparation.

Daily Interactive Pocket Chart Activities: Using the poem text, students will participate in hands-on games and activities that will promote prereading skills, including phonological awareness. Lesson plans for each day focus on essential emergent literacy skills including letter and sound recognition, rhyming, syllabication, basic sight words, and basic punctuation.

Home/School Connection: The week's activities culminate with a fun Home/School Connection activity. A letter pertaining to the weekly theme is included to copy and send home to parents and caregivers. This letter invites parents to take an active role in their children's learning by assisting in a prereading activity, thus fostering literacy development. This letter will encourage parent involvement and extend learning into the home.

Student Poem Page: A page containing the unit's poem, with ample room for children's illustrations, is included. Use this page to help develop fine motor skills, left-to-right correspondence, and oral language.

Mini Book: The Mini Book for each poem will allow children interactive practice with books and book parts such as reading from front-to-back, left-to-right, and top-to-bottom. The end of each Mini Book contains a simple activity that will provide children the opportunity to interact with the poem's text.

Literature Links: A list of related children's literature is included to complement the unit, and help generate and retain interest in the unit's theme.

How to Use This Book

Before you begin each lesson, you will need to gather some supplies. A basic pocket chart with ten pockets will be needed to hold the pocket chart cards. Pocket charts are available at most teacher supply stores and will be an asset to your early childhood classroom by giving your students many opportunities to interact with print. You may also wish to invest in a pocket chart stand to provide quick, rollaway storage for your pocket chart. You will need a few basic office supplies to prepare and complete each lesson, including scissors, crayons, a stapler, tape, and markers.

Prior to starting each unit, you will need to prepare each of the following:

1. Reproduce the Home/School Connection Letter for each student. Go over the activity with your class before sending it home to be sure they understand what they are being asked to do with their parents. You may want to offer a special reward (sticker or small toy) for children who complete the activity.

2. Cut out the Pocket Chart Cards and Picture Cards for the unit. You may want to laminate the cards or attach them to tagboard for durability since all of the activities are hands-on and the cards will be handled a great deal. You can color the Picture Cards if you wish, just be certain you have read the entire unit first to determine if there are any special color requirements for the pictures. Numbering the cards in the correct order and storing them in a large envelope or resealable, plastic bag will help with organization and management of each poem. Commercial sentence strip file boxes can also be purchased at your local teacher supply store.

3. Reproduce and assemble a poem Mini Book for each student. Copy the pages, cut them out, and put them in order. Staple the pages on the left-hand side to create a small book version of the poem for each child to take home. Encourage the children to read their books to their families and friends at home.

4. Reproduce the Student Poem Page for each child. After the children have illustrated the page, hold on to it. Once several units are complete, you may want to compile these individual pages into a booklet for each child to take home periodically and read to his or her family. Using an inexpensive folder for three-hole-punched paper will allow you to add additional poems to the booklets as you complete them.

   Make a mini pointer for the poem collection folder. Attach a 12" string or piece of yarn to one end of a craft stick. Tie the other end of the string or yarn to a ring in the folder. Children can use the pointer to point to the words as they read each poem.

   At the end of the year, give each child a large sheet of folded construction paper to decorate and use as a cover. Staple to poems inside. Save the original mini-binders to use again next year.

5. You may wish to find the Literature Links or other books on the theme in your school or neighborhood library. Reading these books will help generate interest and extend the knowledge the children gain from the unit. Keep the books in an accessible reading area once they have been introduced to students.

   Optional: Each unit begins with a full-page copy of the poem. These pages can be enlarged, colored, and displayed in the classroom. Another option is to copy the pages and create a book for the class library once all the poems have been shared.

 # Teddy Bears

Teddy Bear Red is on the bed.

Teddy Bear Blue is on the shoe.

Teddy Bear Yellow is on the marshmallow.

Teddy Bear Green is on the bean.

Teddy Bear Black is on the track.

Teddy Bear Brown is on the crown.

Teddy Bear Pink is on the sink.

Teddy Bear Gray is on the hay.

Teddy Bears

Unit Preparation

Copy and send home the Teddy Bears Home/School Connection Parent Letter and Homework Page (pages 8–9). Copy and cut apart the Teddy Bears Pocket Chart Cards (pages 10–19). Copy, appropriately color, and cut apart the Teddy Bears Picture Cards (pages 20–21). Place all the cards in the pocket chart in the correct places. Copy the Teddy Bears Student Poem Page (page 22) and *Teddy Bears* Mini Book pages (pages 23–27) for each child. See page 4 for additional preparation tips.

Student Poem Page

Teddy bears are usually brown, but they can also be pink, blue, black, white, and many other colors. Ask the children what colors of teddy bears they have seen. Also review the *Goldilocks and the Three Bears* story with students. Remind students of the big, medium, and little bear in the story. Ask the children what sizes teddy bears come in.

Ask the children to choose their favorite teddy bear and draw a picture of it on the Teddy Bears Student Poem Page. Guide them in writing the teddy bear's color on the blank line on the poem page, or write it for them.

Group the Teddy bears by color. Graph the number of Teddy bears in each color.

Mini Book

Assemble a *Teddy Bears* Mini Book for each child. Have the children color the pages and read their mini books to others. At the end of the week, invite each child to take his or her mini book home and read it to his or her family.

Literature Links

Brown Bear, Brown Bear, What Do You See? by Bill Martin Jr. (Henry Holt and Company, 1996)

Corduroy by Don Freeman (Puffin Books, 1976)

My Friend Bear by Jez Alborough (Candlewick Press, 1998)

Teddy Bear, Teddy Bear: A Classic Action Rhyme
(Harper Festival, 1997)

Teddy Bear's Picnic by Jerry Garcia (HarperCollins, 1996)

Pocket Chart Activities

Monday: Introduce the Poem

Read the poem, "Teddy Bears," aloud to the children. Reread the poem, pointing to the words as you go. Invite the children to read the poem aloud with you. Encourage children to look at their own clothes and note which colors they are wearing.

Tuesday: Color Me

Invite the children to help you recite the poem aloud, pointing to the words as you go. Remove the color words from the poem. Hand the color words out to the children. Read the poem slowly line by line, stopping at the spaces where the color words belong.

Have the whole class look at the pictures to determine which cards are missing on each line. Ask the students to look at their cards to see if they have the missing color word. Invite them to replace the color words, then read the poem together again.

Wednesday: "Beary" Good B's

Invite individual students to find words in the poem beginning with the letter **b**. When they have correctly identified a **b** word, they may remove it from the poem. Read the poem together, pausing for children to replace the missing words as you come to them. Repeat this activity several times until each child has had a turn.

Thursday: Rhyme Time

Discuss rhyming words with the children. Read the poem together and ask them to listen for words that rhyme. Remove the last word of each line in the poem and spread them out in front of you. Reread the poem, stopping each time you come to a missing word. Have the students help find the missing words by looking at the beginning letters of each.

Friday: Culminating Activity

Invite the children to bring their teddy bears, rhyming objects, and Homework Pages to circle time. Ask them to take turns sharing their teddy bears, naming the rhyming objects, and reading their sentences aloud. When they are finished, invite them to have their teddy bears sit or stand on the rhyming objects, as the sentences suggest. Reread the poem together one more time.

Teddy Bears

Teddy Bear Red is on the bed.
Teddy Bear Blue is on the shoe.
Teddy Bear Yellow is on the marshmallow.
Teddy Bear Green is on the bean.
Teddy Bear Black is on the track.
Teddy Bear Brown is on the crown.
Teddy Bear Pink is on the sink.
Teddy Bear Gray is on the hay.

Hello,

This week we will be learning this poem about teddy bears. Using the poem as a springboard, we will be working with rhyming words, color words, and words beginning with the letter **b.** Please read the poem with your child to help him or her learn it.

Please have your child choose a teddy bear from home and draw a picture of it on the *Teddy Bears* Homework Page. (If your child does not have a teddy bear in the color he or she chooses, your child may draw a picture of it.) Once the teddy bear has been selected, help your child find an object rhyming with the color of the bear, or think of an object and draw a picture of it on the Homework Page.

Finally, please help your child fill in the first blank of the sentence with the color of his or her teddy bear. The second blank should be completed with the name of the rhyming object. Please send the teddy bear, rhyming object, and Homework Page to school on _____.

Your child will be bringing home a *Teddy Bears* Mini Book of this week's poem. Please ask him or her to read it to you. Your child may also want to read it to a special friend or relative.

Thank you "beary" much for your participation!

Sincerely,

_____

Homework Page

~~~~~~

Directions: Choose a teddy bear and draw a picture of it in the box. Help your child find an object rhyming with the color of the bear, or think of an object, and draw a picture of it below the bear.

Fill in the first blank of the sentence with the color of your child's teddy bear. The second blank should be completed with the name of the rhyming object.

Teddy Bear _____

is on the _____.

Bears

Bear

is

Teddy

Teddy

Red

the

Teddy

Blue

on

bed.

Bear

on

shoe.

Bear

is

the

Teddy

is

the

marshmallow.

Yellow

on

Bear

is

the

Teddy

Green

on

Teddy

Black

on

bean.

Bear

is

track.

Bear

is

the

Teddy

Brown

the

Teddy

Pink

on

crown.

Bear

on

sink.

Bear

is

the

Teddy

is

the

Gray

on

hay.

Teddy Bears

Teddy Bear Red is on the bed.

Teddy Bear Blue is on the shoe.

Teddy Bear Yellow is on the marshmallow.

Teddy Bear Green is on the bean.

Teddy Bear Black is on the track.

Teddy Bear Brown is on the crown.

Teddy Bear Pink is on the sink.

Teddy Bear Gray is on the hay.

Teddy Bear _____

By:_____

Teddy Bear Red is on the bed.

Teddy Bear Blue is on the shoe.

Teddy Bear Yellow is on the marshmallow.

Teddy Bear Green is on the bean.

Teddy Bear Black is on the track.

Teddy Bear Brown is on the crown.

Teddy Bear Pink is on the sink.

Teddy Bear Gray is on the hay.   **8**

Find the word "on" on each page and circle it.   **9**

Leaves

Leaves are falling

From the ABC tree.

Look very closely,

What do you see?

Uppercase letters,

They are big and tall.

Lowercase letters,

They are very small.

Leaves

Unit Preparation

Copy and send home the Leaves Home/School Connection Parent Letter and Homework Page (pages 31–32). Copy and cut apart the Leaves Pocket Chart Cards (pages 33–37). Copy, color, and cut out the Leaves Picture Cards (pages 38–39). Place all the cards in the pocket chart in the correct places. Copy the Leaves Student Poem Page (page 40) and *Leaves* Mini Book pages (pages 41–45) for each child. Copy, color, and cut out the Leafy Letters (pages 46–50). See page 4 for additional preparation tips.

Student Poem Page

Discuss leaves with the children. Tell them that leaves grow on trees, fall to the ground, and then we rake them up. In the fall, leaves change color from green to red, orange, yellow, or brown. Talk about how the change in temperature to cooler weather causes this change.

Ask the children to decide if they like uppercase or lowercase letters better. Guide them in writing the appropriate word on the blank line on the Leaves Student Poem Page, or write it for them. Allow the children time to illustrate the poem in the space provided.

Note to Teacher: In some settings, uppercase letters are referred to as capital letters. In this book, the term *uppercase* will be used.

Mini Book

Assemble a *Leaves* Mini Book for each child. Have the children color the pages and read their books to others. At the end of the week, invite each child to take the book home and read it to his or her family.

Literature Links

Clifford's First Autumn by Norman Bridwell (Scholastic, 1997)

Fall Leaves Fall by Zoe Hall (Scholastic, 2000)

The Fall of Freddie the Leaf by Leo Buscaglia (Slack, 20th Anniversary Edition, 2002)

I Am a Leaf by Jean Marzollo (Scholastic, 1999)

Red Leaf, Yellow Leaf by Lois Ehlert (Harcourt Children's Books, 1991)

Pocket Chart Activities

Monday: Introduce the Poem

Read the poem, "Leaves," aloud to the children. Reread the poem, pointing to the words as you go. Invite the children to read the poem aloud with you. Talk about different kinds of leaves.

Tuesday: Match-up Madness

Spread the Leafy Letters out on the floor. Show the children that the uppercase letters are large and the lowercase letters are small. Explain that each letter of the alphabet has both an uppercase and a lowercase shape. Demonstrate finding and matching an uppercase and lowercase letter pair. Read the addition to the poem below to the class as they take turns finding and matching the uppercase and lowercase Leafy Letters. After all of the leaves have been matched, ask each child to show his or her matching pair to the class and read the letters aloud saying, "uppercase *A* and lowercase *a*."

> Pick up a big leaf, look at what you found.
>
> Then find the small leaf, the match is on the ground.
>
> Match all the letters, don't stop until you're done.
>
> Learn how to match them, and you'll have lots of fun!

Wednesday: Uppercase Letter Hunt

Invite the children to help you recite the poem aloud, pointing to the words as you go. Ask a child to come forward and find a word containing an uppercase letter in the poem. Ask the child to identify the uppercase letter and then assist him or her in reading the word. Ask the child to take the card back with him or her. Continue in this manner until all of the words containing uppercase letters have been removed. Reread the poem, pausing where each missing word belongs. Ask the child who has the missing word to replace it and continue until the poem has been reassembled. Reread the poem together one more time.

Thursday: Phoneme Categorization

In phoneme categorization, children can identify a word in a set of words that has a different sound. In the following example, identify the beginning sound that is different.

Teacher: Which word doesn't belong in this set: *dog, hat, dad?*

Students: *Hat* doesn't belong, it does not begin with /d/.

Read each of the following sets of words aloud (*falling, you, from; they, do, the; look, tall, small; leaves, letters, big*). Ask the children to identify which word does not belong according to its beginning or ending sound. After the odd word has been identified, have a child help you find each of the words in the poem and identify the matching beginning or ending letters of each.

Friday: Culminating Activity

Invite the children to bring their *Leaves* Homework Pages to the circle. Ask the children which letters they put on their trees. Ask the class to decide if all of the uppercase letters were correctly put on their trees. Next, review which letters the children put on the ground. Again, ask if all of the lowercase letters were put in the correct place on their pages. Reread the poem together one last time to wrap up the unit.

Leaves

Leaves are falling
From the ABC tree.
Look very closely,
What do you see?
Uppercase letters,
They are big and tall.
Lowercase letters,
They are very small.

Hello,

This week we will be learning this poem about leaves. Using the poem as a springboard, we will be working with identifying and matching lowercase and uppercase letters, and identifying different beginning and ending sounds in a group of words (phoneme categorization) throughout the week. Please read the poem with your child to help him or her learn the words.

Please help your child cut out the leaves on the attached Homework Page. On a separate piece of paper, assist your child in drawing a tree with branches, but no leaves. Ask your child to look at each leaf and determine if the letter on it is an uppercase or lowercase letter. Attach each uppercase letter to the tree and each lowercase letter to the ground below the tree with tape or glue. Please send the completed tree to school on _____. (Don't "leaf" home without it!)

Your child will be bringing home a *Leaves* Mini Book of the poem this week. Please ask him or her to read it to you. Your child may also want to read it to a special friend or relative.

Thank you for your participation!

Sincerely,

_____

Homework Page

Directions: Cut out the leaves.

Draw a tree with branches, but no leaves, on a separate sheet of paper.

Using tape or glue, attach each *uppercase* letter leaf to the tree and each *lowercase* letter leaf to the ground below the tree.

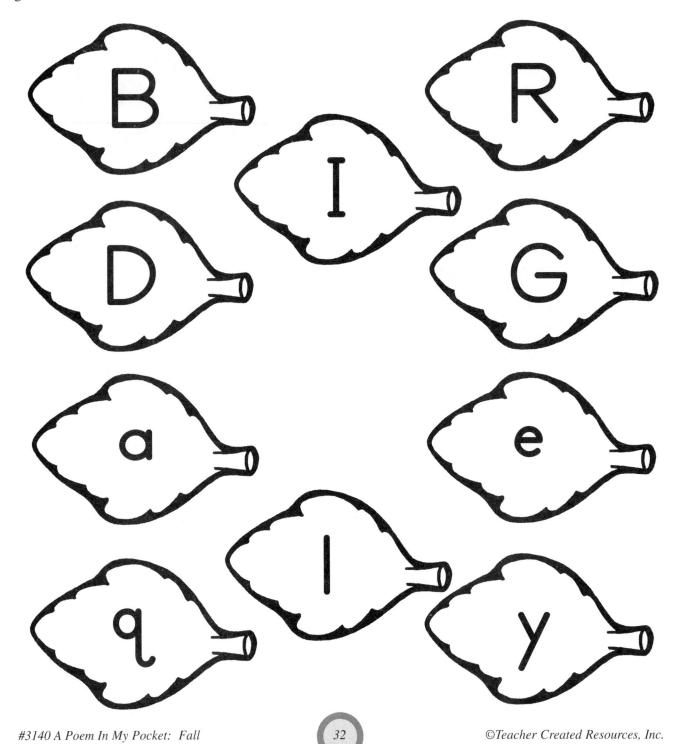

Leaves

falling

the

Leaves

are

From

tree.

very

What

ABC

Look

closely?

you

letters,

do

see?

Uppercase

are

and

They

big

Lowercase

letters,

are

small.

tall.

They

very

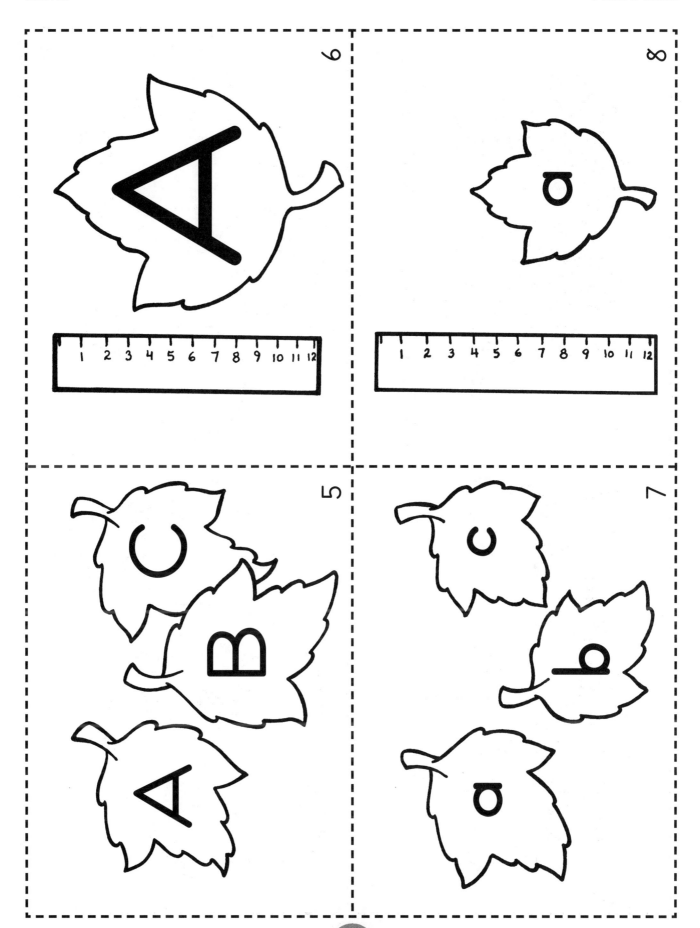

Leaves

Leaves are falling

From the ABC tree.

Look very closely,

What do you see?

Uppercase letters,

They are big and tall.

Lowercase letters,

They are very small.

I like _____ letters the best.

Leaves

By:_____

Leaves are falling

1

From the ABC tree.

2

Look very closely,

3

What do you see?

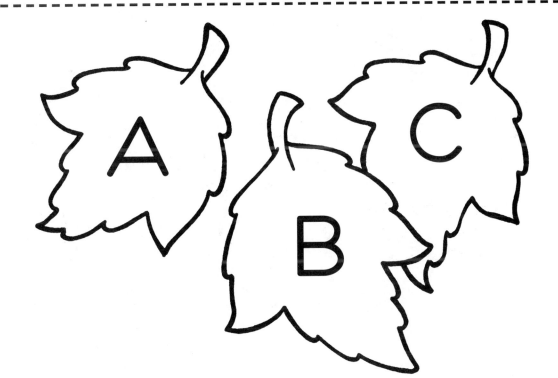

Uppercase letters,

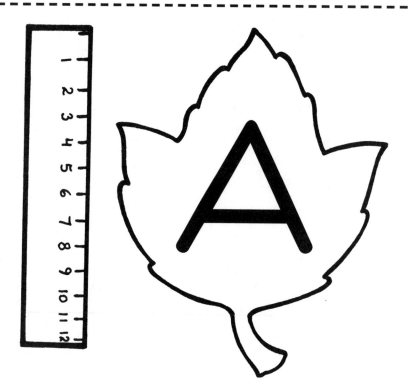

They are big and tall.

Lowercase letters,

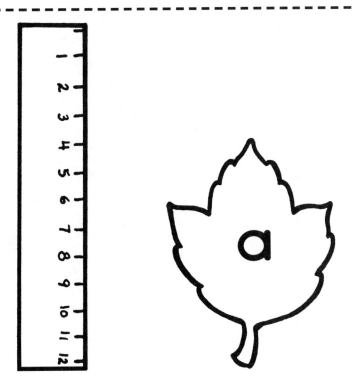

They are very small.   **8**

Find all the UPPERCASE LETTERS
in this book and underline them.   **q**

Leafy Letters

Note to Teacher: Use the Leafy Letters (pages 46–50) for the Match-up Madness activity on page 30.

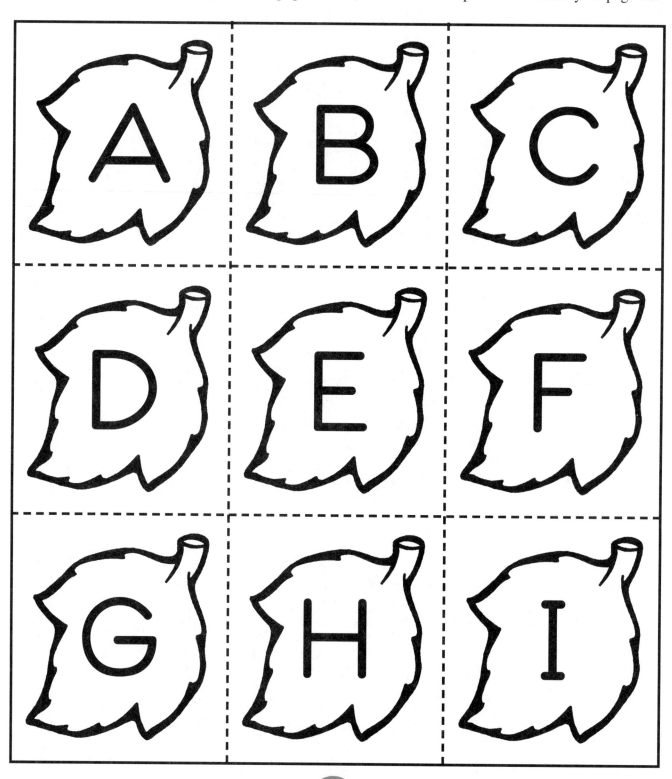

Leafy Letters *(cont.)*

Note to Teacher: Use the Leafy Letters (pages 46–50) for the Match-up Madness activity on page 30.

Leafy Letters *(cont.)*

Note to Teacher: Use the Leafy Letters (pages 46–50) for the Match-up Madness activity on page 30.

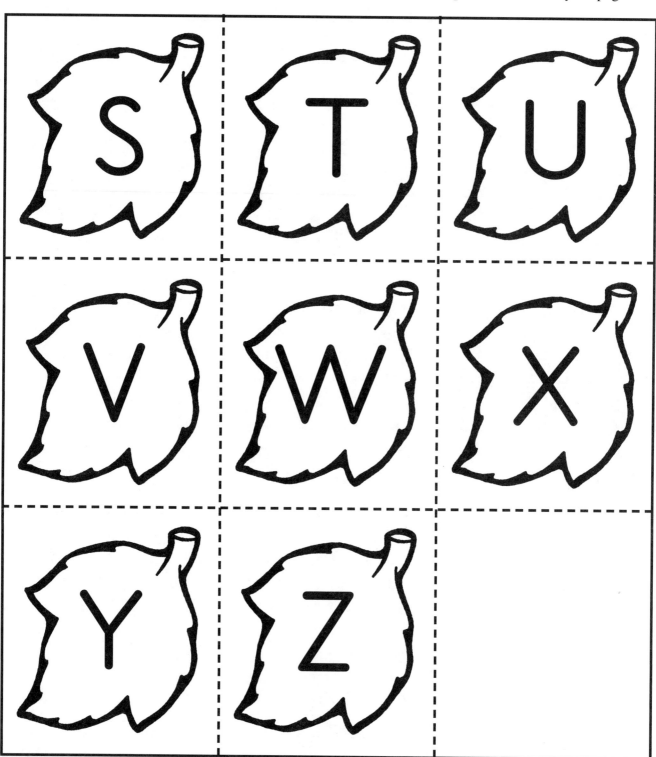

Leafy Letters *(cont.)*

Note to Teacher: Use the Leafy Letters (pages 46–50) for the Match-up Madness activity on page 30.

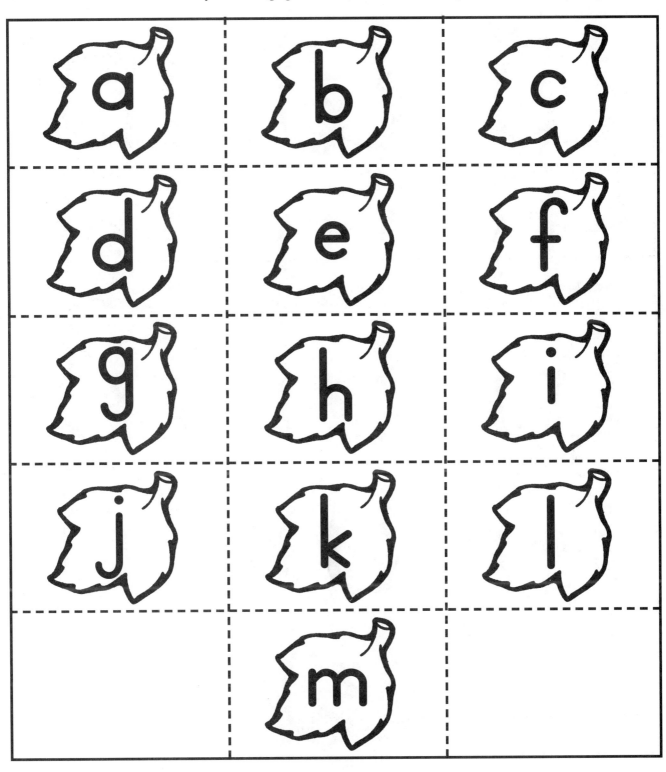

Leafy Letters *(cont.)*

Note to Teacher: Use the Leafy Letters (pages 46–50) for the Match-up Madness activity on page 30.

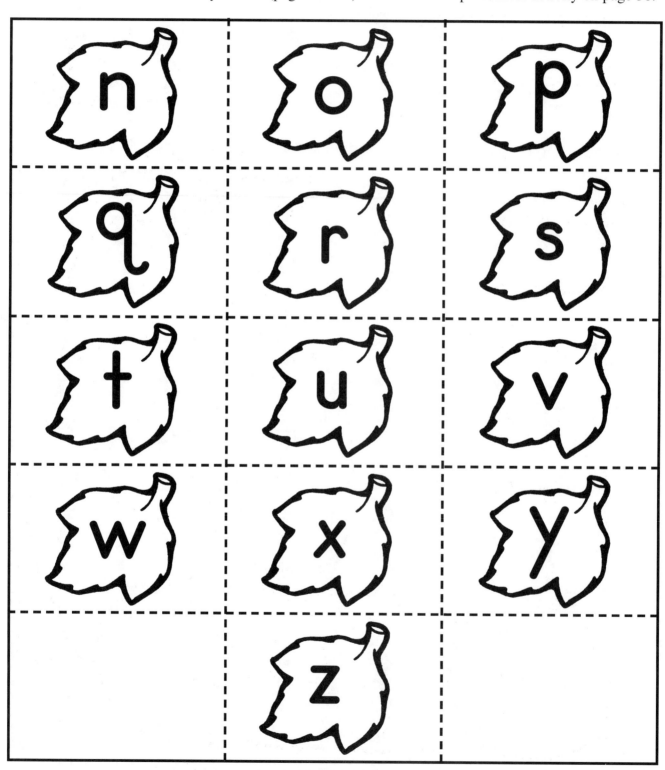

Pumpkins

Three orange pumpkins

Sitting on the ground.

The small one is

Shiny and round.

The medium one is

Wide and flat.

The large one is

Bumpy and fat.

Pumpkins

Unit Preparation

Copy and send home the Pumpkins Home/School Connection Parent Letter and Homework Page (pages 54–55). Copy and cut apart the Pumpkins Pocket Chart Cards (pages 56–60). Copy, color, and cut out the Pumpkins Picture Cards (pages 61–62). Place all the cards in the pocket chart in the correct places. Copy the Pumpkins Student Poem Page (page 63) and *Pumpkins* Mini Book pages (pages 64–68) for each child. See page 4 for additional preparation tips.

Student Poem Page

Discuss with the children if they have ever visited a pumpkin patch. Ask them if they saw *small, medium,* or *large* pumpkins growing. Were the pumpkins round, oval, tall, or short? Were the pumpkins bumpy, rough, or smooth? What colors were the pumpkins?

Ask the children to think of two words to describe what kind of pumpkins they would like to have. Explain that they may choose words that tell about the size, shape, color, or texture of their pumpkins. Assist the children in writing the words in the blanks at the bottom of their Pumpkins Student Poem Pages, or write them for them. Allow the children time to illustrate the poem in the space provided.

Mini Book

Assemble a *Pumpkins* Mini Book for each child. Have the children color the pages and read their books to others. At the end of the week, invite each child to take the book home and read it to his or her family.

Literature Links

The Biggest Pumpkin Ever by Steven Kroll (Cartwheel Books, Reissue Edition, 1993)

The Pumpkin Book by Gail Gibbons (Holiday House, 2000)

Pumpkin Jack by Will Hubbel (Albert Whitman and Co., 2000)

Pumpkin Soup by Helen Cooper (Farrar, Straus and Giroux, 1999)

Too Many Pumpkins by Linda White (Holiday House, Reprint Edition, 1997)

Pocket Chart Activities

Monday: Introduce the Poem

Read the poem, "Pumpkins," aloud to the children. Reread the poem, pointing to the words as you go. Invite the children to read the poem aloud with you. Ask the children to identify each of the pumpkins mentioned.

Tuesday: Size It Up

Invite the children to help you recite the poem aloud, pointing to the words as you go. Remove the words *small, medium,* and *large* from the poem. Remove the pictures of the small, medium, and large pumpkins from the chart. Lay the words and pictures on the floor in front of the children. Ask the children if anyone can read any of the words on the floor. Ask a volunteer to read a word and then find the pumpkin that goes with it, placing them together on the floor. After the words and pumpkins have been matched, reread the poem, pausing where each missing word and picture belong. Ask a volunteer to find the missing word or picture and replace it as you go. When the poem has been reassembled, reread the poem together.

Wednesday: Phoneme Deletion

Phoneme deletion involves children's abilities to recognize a new word when a phoneme has been removed from the original word. For example:

Teacher: What is *flake* without the /f/?

Students: *Flake* without the /f/ is *lake.*

Read each of the following words from the poem in this manner (*ground, small, fat*). After each new word has been determined, ask a child to find the original word in the pocket chart, remove it, and cover the first letter with his or her hand. The class can then verify that the new word is correct by reading the remaining "new" word together.

Thursday: Tiny to Gigantic

After the class is familiar with small, medium, and large, ask them to help you think of other words for small and large (*giant, tiny, itsy-bitsy, huge).* Write each word on a note card or sentence strip that has been cut into pieces large enough for one word, and hand it to the child who came up with it. After the class has contributed several options, read the poem, replacing *small* and *large* with the new words in the pocket chart. Repeat this process until all the new words have been used.

Friday: Culminating Activity

Invite the children to bring their Pumpkin Homework Pages to the circle. Give each child an opportunity to share the small, medium, and large objects they found at home. Encourage the children to use the words *small, medium,* and *large* as they share. Reread the poem one more time to wrap up the unit.

Pumpkins

Three orange pumpkins
Sitting on the ground.
The small one is
Shiny and round.
The medium one is
Wide and flat.
The large one is
Bumpy and fat.

Hello,

This week we will be learning this poem about pumpkins. Using the poem as a springboard, we will be working with words that indicate size (*small, medium, large, tiny, giant,* etc.), as well as deleting sounds from a word to form a new word (phoneme deletion). (For example: *ground* without the /g/ is *round.*) Please read the poem with your child to help him or her learn it.

Please help your child find two sets of objects in your house that come in three sizes (socks, cups, bowls, pants, etc.). After you have gathered the two sets of objects, have your child put them in order from smallest to largest and then draw each in the appropriate space on the attached Pumpkins Homework Page. Please send the completed homework to school on_____.

Your child will be bringing home a *Pumpkins* Mini Book of the poem this week. Please ask him or her to read it to you. Your child may also want to read it to a special friend or relative.

Thank you for making this project a "huge" success!

Sincerely,

_____

Homework Page

Directions: Find two objects in your home that come in three different sizes (socks, cups, bowls, pants, etc.). Have your child place the sets in order from smallest to largest.

Draw each object in the appropriate space.

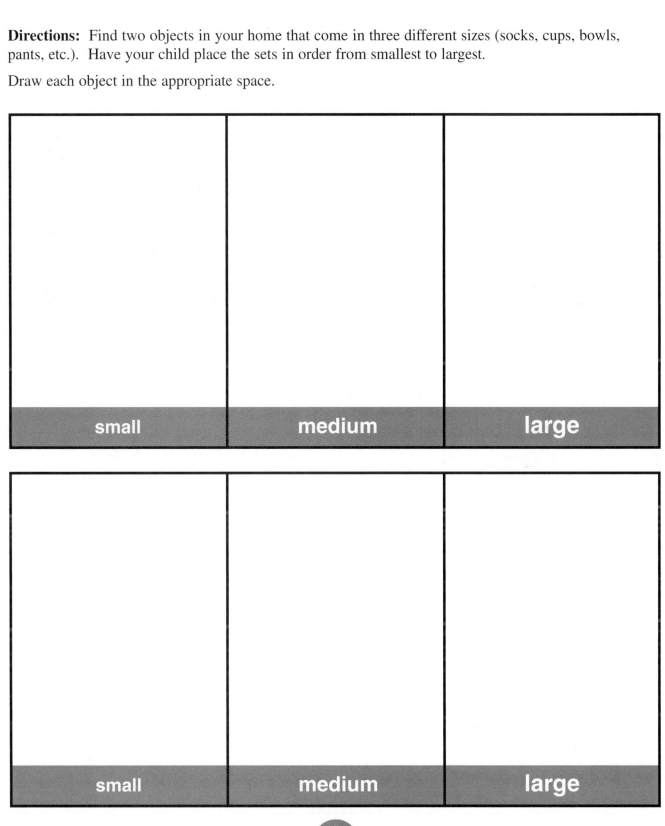

small	medium	large

small	medium	large

Pumpkins

orange

Sitting

Three

pumpkins

the

The

one

on

ground.

small

Shiny

round.

medium

is

and

The

is

and

The

one

Wide

flat.

one

Bumpy

fat.

large

is

and

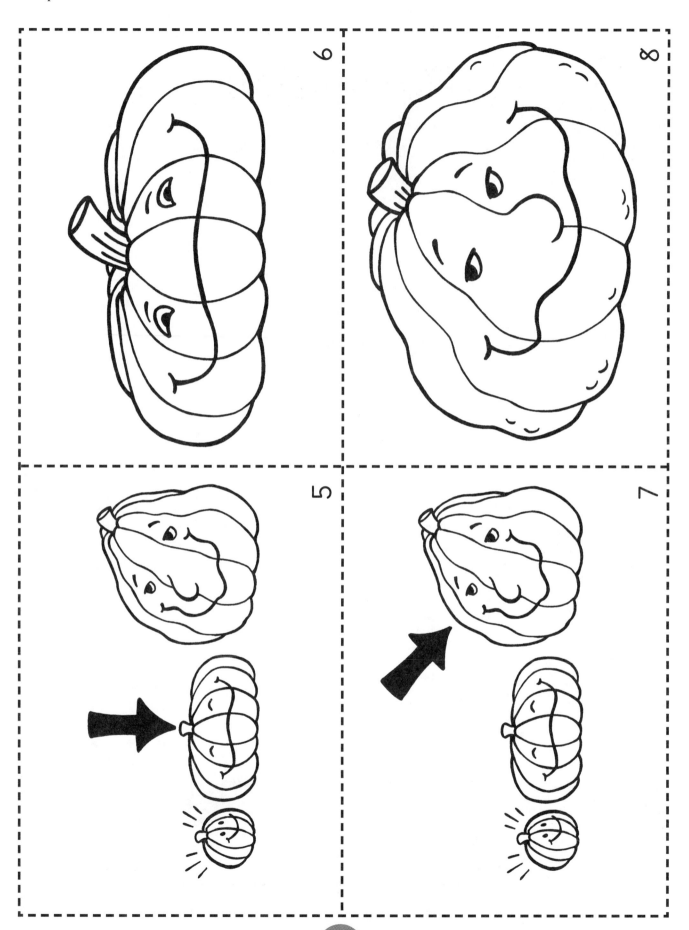

Pumpkins

Three orange pumpkins,

Sitting on the ground.

The small one is

Shiny and round.

The medium one is

Wide and flat.

The large one is

Bumpy and fat.

I would like a _____, _____ pumpkin.

Pumpkins

By:_____

Three orange pumpkins

Sitting on the ground.

The small one is

Shiny and round.

④

The medium one is

⑤

Wide and flat.　　　　　　　　⑥

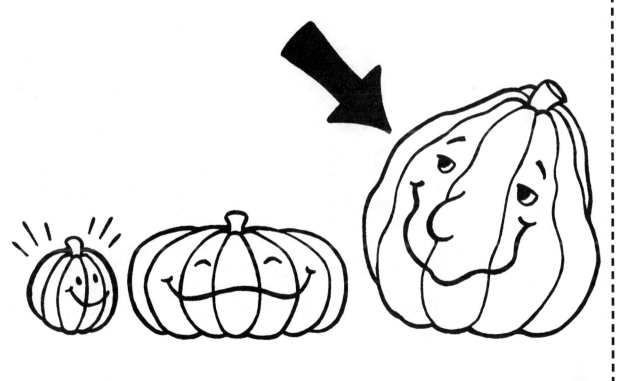

The large one is　　　　　　　⑦

Bumpy and fat. **8**

Find the word "is" and circle it. **9**

The Nut Hunt

The squirrels are on a nut hunt,

For winter is on the way.

Mrs. Squirrel finds 1, 2, 3.

There is no time to play.

Baby Squirrel finds 4 nuts.

Mr. Squirrel finds 5.

6, 7, 8, 9, 10 nuts

Will keep them all alive.

The Nut Hunt

Unit Preparation

Copy and send home The Nut Hunt Home/School Connection Parent Letter and Homework Page (pages 72–73). Copy and cut apart The Nut Hunt Pocket Chart Cards (pages 74–81). Copy, color, and cut apart The Nut Hunt Picture Cards (pages 84–85). Place all the cards in the pocket chart in the correct places. If your class is already familiar with numbers, you may choose to use the Number Word Cards (pages 82–83) instead. Copy The Nut Hunt Student Poem Page (page 86) and *The Nut Hunt* Mini Book pages (pages 87–91) for each child. Copy, color, and cut out The Nut Hunt Patterns (pages 92–93). See page 4 for additional preparation tips.

Student Poem Page

Tell the children that squirrels gather and store nuts in the fall in preparation for the winter. Squirrels store nuts in holes in the ground, in holes in trees, or in their dens. The squirrels find most of the nuts on the ground, not in trees. Because the nuts are scattered, squirrels must search to find them. They eat a lot of nuts before winter so they can live through times when food won't be as easy to get.

Ask the children to write the numbers 1–10 on the blank lines on The Nut Hunt Student Poem Page using the numbers in the poem's text as a guide. Allow the children time to illustrate the poem in the space provided.

Mini Book

Assemble *The Nut Hunt* Mini Book for each child. Have the children color the pages and read their mini books to others. At the end of the week, invite each child to take the book home and read it to his or her family.

Literature Links

Gray Squirrel's Day by Geri Harrington (McGraw Hill Children's Publishing, 2001)

Nuts to You by Lois Ehlert (Harcourt Children's Books, 1993)

Squirrel Is Hungry by Satoshi Kitamura (Farrar, Straus and Giroux, 1996)

Squirrels by Brian Wildsmith (Oxford University Press, 1984)

A Squirrel's Tale by Richard Fowler (Educational Development Corporation, 1984)

Pocket Chart Activities

Monday: Introduce the Poem

Read the poem, "The Nut Hunt," aloud to the children. Reread the poem, pointing to the words as you go. Invite the children to read the poem aloud with you. Ask who has seen squirrels in trees.

Tuesday: Nutty Numbers

Invite the children to help you recite the poem aloud, pointing to the words as you go. Remove the numbers from the poem and spread them out on the floor in front of the class. Read the poem together slowly, pausing at each space where a number belongs. Ask for a volunteer to find the missing number on the floor and place it in the correct place in the pocket chart. Continue until all of the numbers have been replaced. After the children are familiar with the numbers, you may want to repeat this activity using the number words (pages 82–83) in place of the numbers.

Wednesday: Phoneme Isolation

In phoneme isolation, children are able to identify individual sounds in a word. In this activity, children will practice identifying the ending sound of words. Read each of the following words from the poem (*squirrel, nut, winter, on, hunt, will, keep, them, all, nuts*) as in the example below:

    Teacher: What is the last sound in *dog?*

    Students: The last sound in *dog* is /g/.

Note to Teachers: Your focus in this activity is the final sound in the word, not the final letter. After the final sound has been identified, ask a child to come up and find the word in the pocket chart. Ask the child to look at the word and identify the letter that makes the ending sound. Share the letter with the class.

Thursday: The Nut Hunt

Remove all of the words from the pocket chart except for the following lines: *Mrs. Squirrel finds, Baby Squirrel finds, Mr. Squirrel finds.* Spread the number words on the floor in front of the class. Ask for three volunteers to play the parts of Mrs. Squirrel, Mr. Squirrel, and Baby Squirrel and give each child the corresponding squirrel pattern (page 92) to go with his or her part. Ask the "squirrels" to close their eyes or briefly leave the room while ten children hide the nuts (page 93) around the room (the nuts need to be visible, not hidden under anything or in a place that is too difficult to find). Ask the "squirrels" to return and find all ten nuts. After they have been found, ask each "squirrel" to find the number word cards on the floor that match the numbers on the nuts that he or she found. The child will then place the appropriate number words in the pocket chart next to the line for his or her squirrel. (For example, Mr. Squirrel finds *three, four, five.*) Have the class read each line of the pocket chart together. You may wish to repeat this activity to give several children an opportunity to be a squirrel.

Friday: Culminating Activity

Invite the children to bring their Squirrels and Nuts Homework Pages to the circle and hold them up for the class to see. Ask the children to switch papers with a friend. Have the children count the objects in each square of the paper to be sure the objects were counted correctly. Allow the children to make any necessary corrections to their papers, then read the poem together one final time.

The Nut Hunt

The squirrels are on a nut hunt,
For winter is on the way.
Mrs. Squirrel finds 1, 2, 3.
There is no time to play.
Baby Squirrel finds 4 nuts.
Mr. Squirrel finds 5.
6, 7, 8, 9, 10 nuts
Will keep them all alive.

Hello,

This week we will be learning this poem about squirrels and nuts. Using the poem as a springboard, we will be working with counting, numbers, number words, and ending sounds of words (phoneme isolation) throughout the week. Please read the poem with your child to help him or her learn it.

Please help your child complete the attached Squirrels and Nuts Homework Page by counting out the indicated number of small objects in each box and attaching them to the page. You may use the same object in each box. Examples of objects that would work might be stickers, toothpicks, paper clips, beans, or noodles. Please send the completed homework to school on _____.

Your child will be bringing home *The Nut Hunt* Mini Book of the poem this week. Please ask him or her to read it to you. Your child may also want to read it to a special friend or relative.

I know I can "count" on you to make this activity a success!

Sincerely,

_____

Homework Page

Directions: Place the correct number of small objects in each box. You could use stickers, toothpicks, paper clips, beans, noodles, etc. Attach the objects to the page using glue or tape.

1	2	3
4	5	6

7	8

9

10

Nut

The

are

The

Hunt

squirrels

a

hunt,

winter

on

nut

For

on

way.

Squirrel

is

the

Mrs.

1,

3.

is

finds

2,

There

time

play.

Squirrel

no

to

Baby

4

Mr.

finds

finds

nuts.

Squirrel

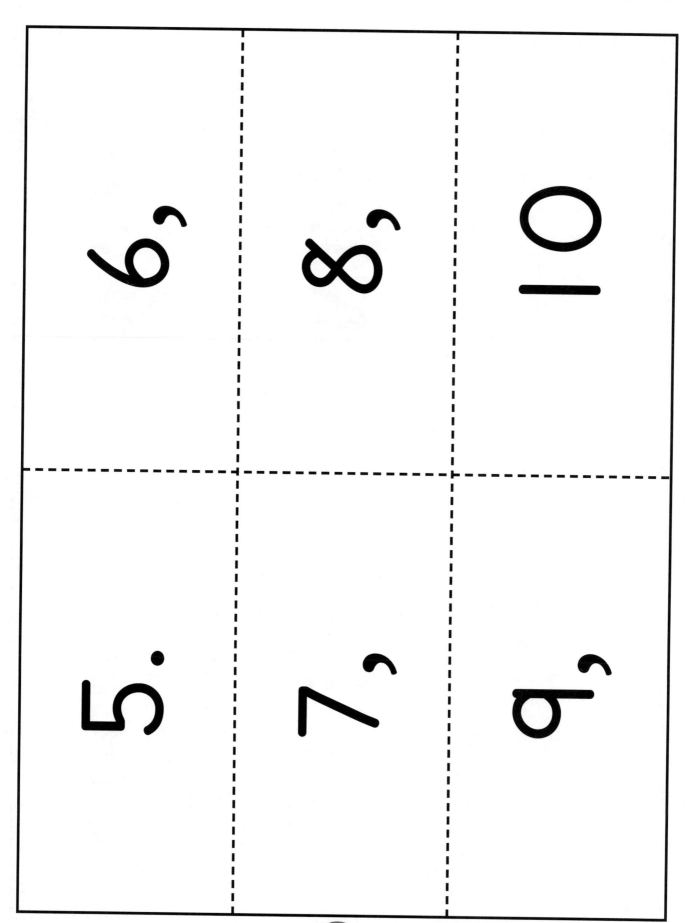

Will

them

alive.

nuts

keep

all

two,

four

Six,

one,

three.

five.

eight,

ten

seven,

nine,

The Nut Hunt

The squirrels are on a nut hunt,

For winter is on the way.

Mrs. Squirrel finds _____, _____, _____.

There is no time to play.

Baby Squirrel finds _____ nuts.

Mr. Squirrel finds _____.

_____, _____, _____, _____, _____ nuts

Will keep them all alive.

1 2 3 4 5 6 7 8 9 10

The Nut Hunt

By:_____

The squirrels are on a nut hunt,

For winter is on the way.

Mrs. Squirrel finds 1, 2, 3.

There is no time to play.   **4**

Baby Squirrel finds 4 nuts.   **5**

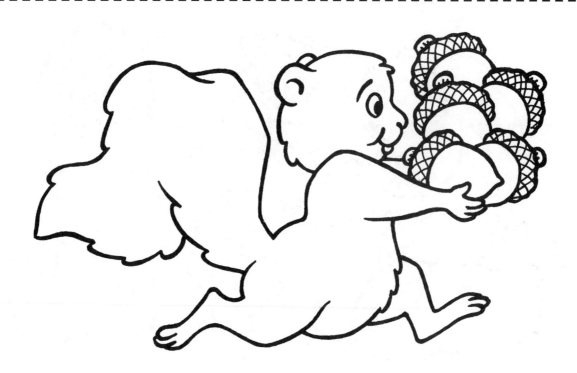

Mr. Squirrel finds 5.

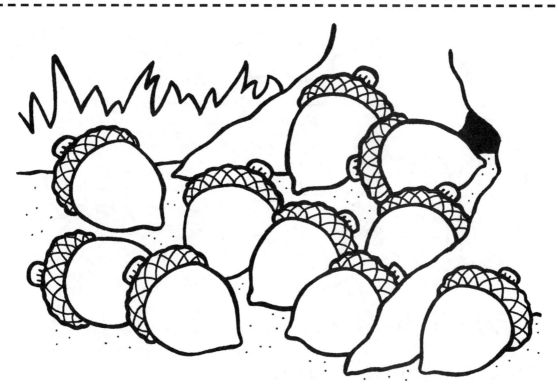

6, 7, 8, 9, 10 nuts

Will keep them all alive.   **8**

Find all the numbers and draw a
circle around them.

1 2 3 4 5 6 7 8 9 10

9

Squirrel Patterns

Note to Teacher: Copy, color, and cut out the Squirrel Patterns. Use with The Nut Hunt activity on page 71.

Nut Patterns

Note to Teacher: Copy, color, and cut out the Nut Patterns. Use with The Nut Hunt activity on page 71.

Apples

Apple Red

Sat on the bed with some bread.

Apple Green

Shared a bean with the queen.

Apple Yellow

Ate some Jell-O with a fellow.

Apple Brown

Fell upside down with a frown.

Apples

Unit Preparation

Copy and send home the Apples Home/School Connection Parent Letter and Homework Page (pages 97–98). Copy and cut apart the Apples Pocket Chart Cards (pages 99–104). Copy, color, and cut apart the Apples Picture Cards (pages 105–106). Place all the cards in the pocket chart in the correct places. Copy the Apples Student Poem Page (page 107) and *Apples* Mini Book pages (pages 108–112) for each child. See page 4 for additional preparation tips.

Student Poem Page

Talk to the children about where apples grow (*on trees, in orchards,* etc.). Ask the children about the colors of apples. Discuss how apples that you would want to eat can be green, red, or yellow. Talk about the foods you can make with apples. Ask children if they have tasted applesauce, apple juice, dried apples, or apple pie. Which food do they like the best?

Ask the children to choose which apple from the poem they would like to draw. Guide them in writing the word on the blank line on the Apples Student Poem Page, or write it for them. Allow the children time to illustrate the poem in the space provided.

Mini Book

Assemble an *Apples* Mini Book for each child. Have the children color the pages and read their books to others. At the end of the week, invite each child to take the book home and read it to his or her family.

Literature Links

Apple Farmer Annie by Monica Wellington (Dutton Children's Books, 2001)

The Apple Pie Tree by Zoe Hall (Scholastic, 1996)

Applesauce by Shirley Kurtz (Good Books, 1992)

The Crooked Apple Tree by Eric Houghton (Barefoot Books, 2000)

Johnny Appleseed by Reeve Lindbergh (Megan Tingley, Reissue edition, 1993)

Pocket Chart Activities

Monday: Introduce the Poem

Read the poem, "Apples," aloud to the children. Reread the poem, pointing to the words as you go. Invite the children to read the poem aloud with you. Vote on the children's favorite apple color.

Tuesday: Rhyme Time

Beforehand, write several words on cards that rhyme with the ending words in each line of the poem. Invite the children to help you recite the poem aloud, pointing to the words as you go. Introduce the idea of rhyming words to the class. Tell them that rhyming words are words that sound the same at the end. Give them several examples (*dog, log, jog; cat, mat, bat*). As you reread the poem, ask the children to raise their hands when they hear words that rhyme. Remove each rhyming word and replace it with another word card that rhymes. After all of the rhyming words have been removed, read each rhyming word set together as a class. Mix up the words on the floor, and reread the poem, pausing where each missing word belongs. Ask for a volunteer to identify and replace each missing word in the pocket chart.

Wednesday: Phoneme Blending

In phoneme blending, children listen to a sequence of individual sounds (or phonemes) and then combine them to form a word. For example:

> **Teacher:** What is this word? /c/ /a/ /t/?

> **Students:** /c/ /a/ /t/ is *cat*.

Read each of the following words from the poem (*red, bed, bread; green, bean, queen; yellow, Jell-O®, fellow; brown, down, frown*) as in the example above. After the children have correctly identified the word, ask for a volunteer to locate the word within the poem's text in the pocket chart and remove it. Hold each word up for the class and point to each letter as you make its sound.
(**Teacher:** /c/ /a/ /t/ are the sounds in *cat*. Now let's read it together. **Students:** cat.)

Thursday: Apple Blue?

Remove all of the words from the pocket chart except the word *apple*. Write the colors *blue, black, pink,* and *white* on note cards or sentence strips. Tell the class you are going to rewrite the poem using some different colors. After the first word *apple*, insert the word *blue*. Next have the children brainstorm ideas of where apple blue might be and what he might be doing. Remind the class of the rhyming pattern of the text. After the class has decided on the new text, write it on sentence strips and place it in the appropriate place in the pocket chart. Repeat this procedure for *black, pink,* and *white* to complete the poem. When your new poem is complete, read it together as a class.

Friday: Culminating Activity

Invite the children to bring their Homework Pages to the circle. Ask each child to share his or her two sets of rhyming objects with the class. After all of the children have had a turn, you may want to further expand on each set of rhyming words by asking the class if they can think of any other words that rhyme with the objects each child picked. Reread the poem together one final time.

Apples

Apple Red
Sat on the bed with some bread.

Apple Green
Shared a bean with the queen.

Apple Yellow
Ate some Jell-O with a fellow.

Apple Brown
Fell upside down with a frown.

Hello,

This week we will be learning this poem about apples. Using the poem as a springboard, we will be working with identifying and creating rhymes, and blending individual sounds to create words (phoneme blending) throughout the week. Please read the poem with your child to help him or her learn it.

Please help your child find two pairs of objects that rhyme. If you are unable to find the objects in your home, your child may draw pictures of them. Draw the rhyming pairs on the attached Homework Page and assist your child in filling in the blanks or write the words for him or her. Send the Homework Page to school on_____.

Your child will be bringing home an *Apples* Mini Book of the poem this week. Please ask him or her to read it to you. Your child may also want to read it to a special friend or relative.

Thank YOU for what you DO!

Sincerely,

_____

Homework Page

Directions: Find two pairs of objects that rhyme. Fill in the blanks and draw each pair in the appropriate box.

_____ rhymes with _____ .

_____ rhymes with _____ .

Apple

Sat

the

Apples

Red

on

with

bread.

Green

bed

some

Apple

a

with

queen.

Shared

bean

the

Yellow

some

with

Apple

Ate

Jell-O

fellow.

Brown

upside

a

Apple

Fell

with

frown.

down

a

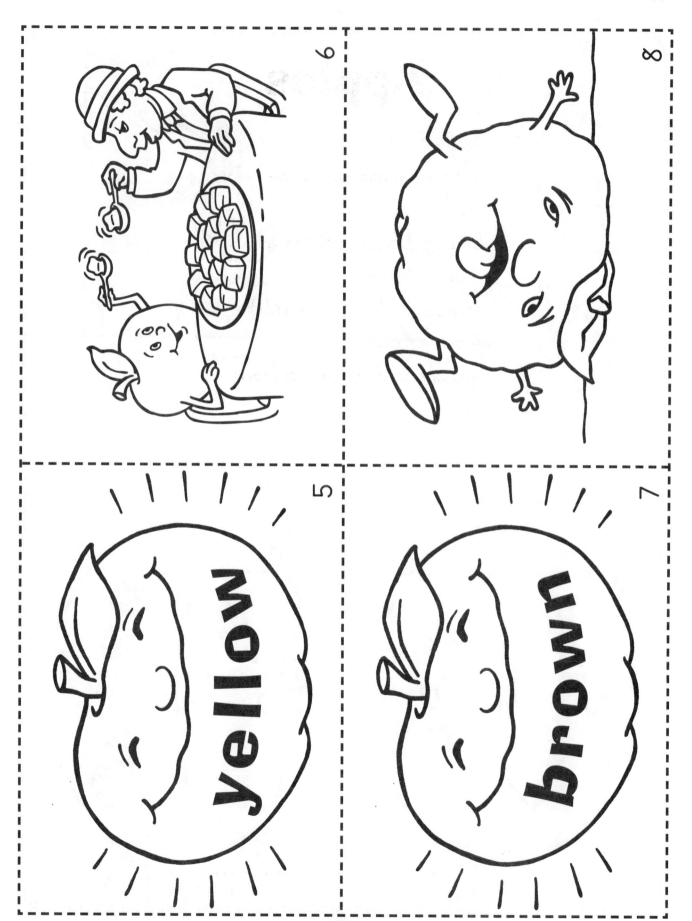

Apples

Apple Red

Sat on the bed with some bread.

Apple Green

Shared a bean with the queen.

Apple Yellow

Ate some Jell-O with a fellow.

Apple Brown

Fell upside down with a frown.

Apple _____

By:_____

Apple Red

Sat on the bed with some bread.

Apple Green   **3**

Shared a bean with the queen.

Apple Yellow

Ate some Jell-O with a fellow. **6**

Apple Brown **7**

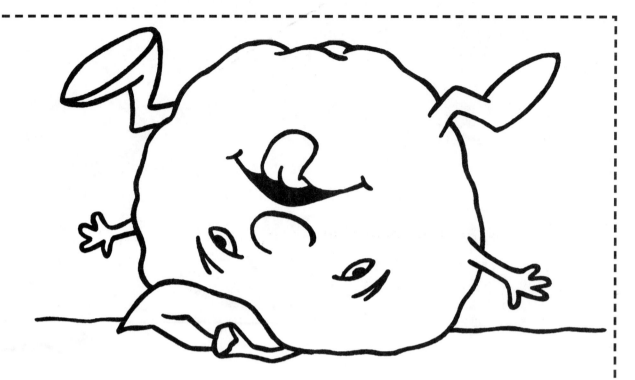

Fell upside down with a frown.

Find the word "with" and underline it.